SCIENCE MADE SIMPLE™

# MOTION AND FORCES

TAMRA ORR

rosen publishing's
rosen central®

New York

Published in 2011 by The Rosen Publishing Group, Inc.
29 East 21st Street, New York, NY 10010

First Edition

**Library of Congress Cataloging-in-Publication Data**

Orr, Tamra.
Motion and forces / Tamra Orr.
    p. cm. — (Science made simple)
Includes bibliographical references and index.
ISBN 978-1-4488-1232-5 (library binding)
ISBN 978-1-4488-2240-9 (pbk.)
ISBN 978-1-4488-2246-1 (6-pack)
1. Motion—Juvenile literature. 2. Force and energy—Juvenile literature.
I. Title.
QC133.5.O77 2011
531'.11—dc22

                                                      2010020535

*Manufactured in Malaysia*

CPSIA Compliance Information: Batch #W11YA: For further information, contact Rosen Publishing, New York, New York, at 1-800-237-9932.

**On the cover:** Top: The world's largest superconducting solenoid magnet (CMS), at the European Organization for Nuclear Research (CERN)'s Large Hadron Collider (LHC) particle accelerator in Geneva. The LHC accelerates sub-atomic particles to nearly the speed of light before smashing them together.
Bottom: Newton's Third Law of Motion, relating to equal and opposite forces, is illustrated every time sprinters push against starting blocks to provide an explosive burst at the start of a race.

# CONTENTS

# INTRODUCTION

When we study certain complex scientific principles and theories, it can sometimes be hard to imagine how they play a part in our daily lives. Motions and forces, however, are everywhere we turn, every single day of our lives.

A force is any kind of a push or a pull. When a person gets up in the morning, it is the force of gravity that keeps her on the ground instead of floating up to the ceiling. When she does her homework, the force of momentum keeps her pencil moving across the paper. When she rides the school bus, it is also momentum that keeps the vehicle moving down the road. Forces put people, their utensils and tools, their vehicles, and even the stars and planets into motion.

Forces are such an essential part of our everyday lives that we usually take them completely for granted. Take gravity, for example. We usually do not give it much thought at all. Yet if it didn't

Knowledge and brain power tell the hand what to write on the page. Yet it is momentum that keeps the pencil moving across the paper.

exist, we would be in big trouble. In fact, we would all find ourselves becoming astronauts—although without the training, the rocket ships, the protective spacesuits, or the oxygen tanks. Gravity is the force that pulls things toward Earth and keeps our feet safely planted on the ground.

Another force that is an important part of our daily reality is friction. This is a force that acts in the opposite direction of an object's motion, serving to slow or halt that object's momentum. It works hard to bring people and objects to a stop. Friction is generated when two surfaces rub against each other. Imagine someone rubbing their hands together vigorously on a cold day. The heat that is generated by this action is the result of friction—the skin of the two hands rubbing against each other. When someone rides a skateboard downhill, there is friction between the wheels and the road. An ice skater experiences a smaller amount of friction between his blades and the ice than a skateboarder does between his wheels and the pavement. Since ice doesn't generate a lot of friction, it is slippery, making it easy for skaters to fall. When the skater steps off the ice and onto the rubber flooring of the rink, he quickly realizes—often by tripping—how much more friction there is off the ice on less slippery surfaces with more grip.

Momentum itself is not a force. It is the product of mass multiplied by velocity. Yet momentum can lead to a force if it is transferred to another body. Depending on how much momentum an object has (and the object's weight), it can mow over anything in its path (a semitrailer traveling at highway speed) or barely make an impact when it hits a person (a slowly rolling soccer ball). Momentum is what makes it hard to stop an object. When someone is racing down the stairs and through the house to make sure he doesn't miss the bus, that person is overflowing with momentum. If he spots some toast on the kitchen table and tries to come to a sudden halt to grab a few bites, he may fall down or slide right past the table. His momentum was too great to allow a sudden stop. The more massive a moving thing is, the more momentum it has and the harder it is to stop. That's why the 300-pound (136-kilogram) linebacker on the football field carries the ball toward the goal line instead of the 100-pound (45 kg) cheerleader. The linebacker has far more mass, so his momentum is much harder to slow or stop.

Inertia is another important force to understand, even though it actually sounds like the absence of force. Imagine someone curled up on the living room couch, watching her favorite TV show. She is interrupted when her mother asks her to take out the trash. She is so comfortable and restful that she doesn't want to move a single inch. Inertia is the tendency for an object to resist change. If it is moving, it does not want to stop, and if it is at rest, it wants to stay at rest. In an empty hamster cage, the hamster wheel is still. It is going to stay that way until a force—the hamster's paws, someone's hand, a strong breeze—comes along to change its inertia and set it into motion. Once it starts spinning, however, the wheel will have a tendency to keep spinning until yet another force, like friction, brings it to a stop.

When getting out of bed in the morning, one should pay close attention to the forces that surround him or her. Gravity is everywhere and constant. But what about other forces and the motions they start, stop, continue, or otherwise affect? Where can we observe friction, momentum, and inertia at work?

# THE BASICS OF MOTION AND FORCES

A force, in scientific terms, means some type of push or pull. Forces cause a change in motion, and each kind of force does its job well. When forces are applied to everything from people to tectonic plates to planets, they create change. They slow things down or speed them up. They change an object's direction or shape. Some create change by coming into direct contact (wind on a scrap of paper). And some do it without contact, from a remote distance (magnets).

If someone wants to observe forces in action, he just has to look around. See the child going down the slide in the park? The force of gravity pushes her down, and the slipperiness of the slide lessens the friction, so she goes faster. See the soccer team practicing out on the field? The goalie

The motion of the wind is a force that keeps windmill blades turning and generating electricity for a growing number of homes and businesses throughout the country.

kicks the ball, and the forces of gravity, air resistance, and friction slow the ball down until it finally stops moving. That tug-of-war going on over at the other end of the park also demonstrates force. Each side is exerting a force, pulling as hard as it can and leaning back to add weight to it. If both sides are equally strong, neither will win. Their force is strong, but they cancel each other out. Even the trail of footprints over in the muddy part of the park has a lesson to teach. Tracks show that the pressure of the person or animal that made them was stronger than the ability of the ground to resist it. If the tracks were made by a cat, they might be light because a cat has little mass. However, just imagine if they had been made by a bulldozer. The tracks would have dug deep into the dirt.

# THE LAWS OF MOTION

The ways that motion and forces work in today's world are understood by us thanks mainly to the work of people like

Galileo Galilei (1564–1642) and Sir Isaac Newton (1643–1727). Galileo conducted a number of experiments that questioned the scientific work of others who had come before him. In the process, he learned a great deal about the way the universe worked. Decades later, Newton took that information and created a set of three laws that explain the key characteristics of forces and motion and what happens when they interact.

Newton's first law of motion concerns inertia. When a car slams on its brakes suddenly and unexpectedly, the passengers experience the potentially jarring effects of friction overcoming inertia. Even though the car has stopped, the passengers' bodies are still in motion. In fact, they are traveling at the same speed the car

Crash test dummies, like this one being thrown from the motorcycle, are proof that when friction overcomes inertia, the results can be jarring—and deadly.

was going before the driver hit the brakes. This is why seatbelts are so essential. They halt the body's potentially fatal and very rapid motion through a suddenly stationary car made of steel and glass. Seatbelts help passengers' bodies overcome inertia by forcibly halting their forward motion and bringing them to a stop. Now the passengers' bodies are again traveling at the same speed as the car—zero miles per hour. A similar sensation can be experienced in an elevator. Like a car, an elevator is a moving object that can experience sudden speeding up, slowing down, or stopping—all changes to the inertia of its present operating speed. When an elevator comes to an abrupt halt on a downward journey, passengers are knocked off their feet or must at least bend their knees to absorb the force of the motion that continues to push them downward. Then they experience the force of inertia again and become as still as the elevator.

These runners are about to burst into motion, but first they have to exert enough energy to overcome their resting bodies' inertia. The starting blocks help them do this by providing an equal and opposite force to that of their feet pushing against the blocks, allowing for an explosive forward thrust.

In his second law, Newton wrote that force is equal to mass times acceleration. If someone dropped a brick and a golf ball from the roof of her school, the two objects would hit the ground at the same time, despite their different weights. Yet

the brick would hit the ground with much more force because of its greater mass. The same principle is at work in a tug-of-war. If both sides have the same number of equal sized people and the pulling force of each person is equal, then the force the two sides generate to pull on the rope will also be equal. But if the wrestling team suddenly joins one side to help out, that side will be able to exert more force since it has gained a lot more mass.

Newton's third law is known as equal and opposite. For every action, there is an equal and opposite reaction. Not sure how this works? Try this. First, blow up a balloon. With the opening held downward, release it. The air in the balloon pushes downward and out the opening. This escaping air sends the balloon flying upward. Similarly, a rocket, powered by the combustion (burning) of gases, sends plumes of flame and gas shooting out from its engines located at its base, while it takes off upward. Watch sprinters "on their marks" just before the starting gun. See the blocks behind their feet that they push against? Why do they do this? The force of the blocks pushing back against their feet provides them with a more powerful forward burst and a faster start.

## OPPOSING MOTION: GRAVITY AND FRICTION

If motions are so powerful, what force can oppose them? Friction and gravity certainly can. Friction acts in a direction that is opposite to the direction an object is taking. And gravity pulls objects toward the ground. Think about ice hockey. There is very little friction between the puck and the surface of the

# Physics at the Ball Game

When you are watching a baseball game, munching on a hot dog, drinking a soda, and hoping for a home run, you may not be thinking about physics (the science of motion) at all. However, if you take a moment to really notice what is happening down on the baseball diamond, you may be surprised at how much you could be learning about motion and forces.

For example, did you see the catcher reach out and halt that fastball in its tracks? It was moving at almost 100 miles an hour (161 kilometers an hour) and yet, one hand, covered in thick leather, was able to stop it in an instant. Where does the force of that ball go? It is absorbed by the mitt. Where else does it go? It is spread out through the catcher's hand, arm, and shoulder. What happens when a player tries to slide into home base and the catcher reaches out to stop him? The force of the base runner's movement comes up against the stationary catcher. It is absorbed—and stopped—by the catcher's body. In each of these examples, motion and momentum are stopped by a stronger force.

Physics is certainly involved on the pitcher's mound as well. Keep an eye on those curve balls. Watch how the pitcher grasps the ball with his middle and index fingers near the ball's stitches. As he throws it, he snaps his wrist. It is a little like reaching out to turn a doorknob. The spin determines the direction the ball moves through the air. What slows it down? The same force that slows a Frisbee—air resistance, a type of resistive force similar to friction.

ice, so what happens? The puck is meeting very little resistance, since ice is smooth. Smooth surfaces generate less friction. So the puck slides quickly from one end of the ice to the other without slowing down very much or changing direction until it hits the boards or is met by a hockey stick. A combination of gravity and air friction brings Frisbees back down to Earth within a few seconds of being tossed. Without either gravity or friction, they would remain spinning and airborne indefinitely, until some other object collided with them to change their speed and direction.

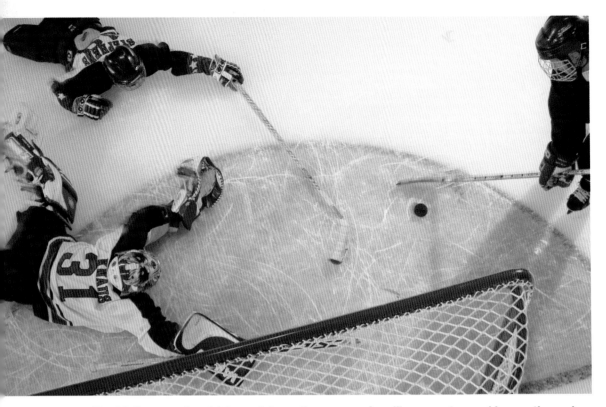

The friction on an ice rink is much lower than on a surface like concrete or rubber, so the puck is able to slide farther and players skate extremely fast.

Forces are largely invisible but incredibly powerful. Understanding how they affect the world around us helps us explain why moving a book from one shelf to another is easy, while moving a refrigerator is harder. It explains why the baseball we threw didn't make it to first base. It also explains why, when we push off from the side of the pool, we are propelled farther than we are when we begin swimming without pushing off. In other words, like most scientific investigations, observing and understanding what motion and forces do in the "real world" makes the universe both a more comprehensible and a more fascinating place.

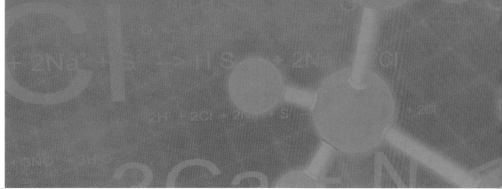

# THE MEN OF MOTION

The *Star Wars* movies may have popularized the phrase "May the Force be with you." But it was men like Galileo Galilei and Isaac Newton who performed so many experiments and made so many observations that they ultimately discovered what the force really was!

## ARGUING WITH ARISTOTLE

Up until Galileo's time, much of the Western world's body of scientific knowledge came from the philosopher Aristotle (384–322 BCE). He came up with a number of theories about how the world worked—some of which were correct and some of which were off-the-mark. For example, Aristotle believed that motion and gravity existed because objects yearned to seek their natural place on the ground, where they could rest.

Galileo disagreed with some of Aristotle's theories even though they had gone unquestioned for more than a thousand years. He was fascinated by how invisible forces within the world affected things. To test his own theories about motion and velocity, he conducted a number of practical experiments.

## HANDS-ON EXPERIMENTS

One of the most famous of these experiments may actually be the stuff of legends and may never have occurred. Known as the Falling Bodies experiment, it was said to have taken place at the Leaning Tower of Pisa in Italy. In order to disprove Aristotle's theory that heavier bodies fall faster than light ones, Galileo dropped a bullet and a cannonball over the edge of the tower and carefully observed how quickly they fell. They allegedly fell at

Whether or not Galileo's experiment at the Leaning Tower of Pisa ever actually happened is not the point. The enduring lesson from the story is that objects of different mass will fall at virtually the same speed, once air resistance is accounted for.

the same rate of speed and landed on the ground at approximately the same time. So objects of different masses will fall at approximately the same rate, Galileo concluded, though air resistance will have some effect on the individual rates of speed.

In another experiment, Galileo rolled a ball down a number of different inclines. He quickly discovered that the speed of a falling object increased as it went downhill. The steeper the incline, the faster the ball gained speed. This taught him even more about gravity, momentum, and falling objects.

## BOLD GUESSES AND GREAT DISCOVERIES

Though Galileo made much progress in understanding motion and forces through these various experiments, it was Newton who expanded on Galileo's ideas and developed what would become one of the most important and enduring systems of scientific laws ever devised. As he once stated, "No great discovery was ever made without a bold guess."

Newton's work discovered and expressed the relationship between force and motion. He proved that any change in motion between two physical objects is due to force acting upon them. Newton correctly theorized that when a lead ball rolls across a wooden floor, it does not stop because it needs to rest. Rather, there is friction between the ball and the floor, which brings it to a halt. Newton was also responsible for realizing that everything was connected by the same force. He named this force gravity, after the word *gravitas*, Latin for "heaviness" or "weight." He published his theories in *Mathematical Principles of Natural Philosophy* in 1687.

## NEWTON'S THREE LAWS OF MOTION

*Mathematical Principles of Natural Philosophy* contained Isaac Newton's most important discoveries regarding forces and

## Galileo's Water Clock

Recording accurate results and observations wasn't easy in the seventeenth century. Since this was long before stopwatches or highly accurate digital timekeepers, Galileo relied on the water clock when conducting his incline experiments. This was a container that he began filling with water the moment the ball began rolling down the incline. As soon as the ball reached the bottom, Galileo halted the flow of water into the water clock. He would then weigh the water that had entered the clock. When the ball rolled down steeper inclines, it traveled faster. Thus less water filled the water clock because there was less time for it to flow. When the ball rolled down a flatter incline, it moved more slowly, meaning more water would have filled the water clock. So Galileo was basically measuring time not by seconds or milliseconds, but by the weight and volume of water.

motion. These came to be known as his three laws of motion. Through these laws, Isaac Newton managed to fundamentally change how people saw the world and how it worked, and how and why all the matter contained within it moved in the ways it did.

The first law states that "every object in a state of uniform motion tends to remain in that state of motion unless an external force is applied to it." This is often referred to as the law of inertia. It basically means that there is a natural tendency for objects to continue doing whatever it is they are currently doing. They resist change. And, if they do not encounter any forces, they will keep right on going as they have been, along the same path and at the same speed.

Newton's second law is complex, but it is considered the most powerful of the three. It states that "the relationship between an object's mass $m$, its acceleration $a$, and the applied force $F$ is F=ma. Acceleration and force are vectors; in this law the direction of the force vector is the same as the direction

Isaac Newton is perhaps best known for his theories of gravity derived from an incident when he was hit on the head by a falling apple. Yet he was also the driving force behind some of physics' most fundamental and important laws.

of the acceleration vector." Basically, the formula states that force is equal to mass times acceleration. This sounds complicated, but it is something that most people understand on an intuitive level. For example, you know that it takes less force to push your pillow from your bed across the floor with your foot than it does to push that laundry basket full of dirty clothes. This is because the pillow's mass is less than that of the full laundry basket. The rate of acceleration may be the same. But since the mass is less, when the two are multiplied together, the result—the force applied to the pillow—is lower than that of the force applied to the higher mass laundry basket.

Newton's third law of motion simply states that "for every action there is an equal and opposite reaction." In other words, for every action a person or object makes, the opposite action occurs with the same amount of force. You can see this law in action when you see a rocket take off. As its ignited engines push downward against the ground, the rocket is pushed upward with equal force. Likewise, if you step off a boat onto a dock, the boat will be pushed backward with the same amount of force that propels you forward.

# CHAPTER

# 3

# FORCES IN MOTION: CONTROVERSY AND CELEBRITY

A nyone who spends time reading and learning about motion and forces is sure to run across the two most important names in the field: Galileo Galilei and Sir Isaac Newton. They discovered and articulated some of the most important principles of physics. Their lives were devoted to figuring out as much about the universe and how it worked as possible.

## CENTER OF THE UNIVERSE

Galileo Galilei was born in Pisa, Tuscany, in Italy. The son of a musician, he decided that he wanted to become a monk. He spent time in the monastery of Santa Maria di Vallombrosa but finally bowed to his father's pressure to study medicine. It did not

Galileo did a great deal to expand people's understanding of the universe. He also created some amazing inventions like this thermometer, known originally as a thermoscope.

take long for him to realize that becoming a doctor was not what he wanted to do with his life. His passion was for mathematics and philosophy. By the age of twenty-one, Galileo had left medical school and studied under a variety of math professors. After teaching at the University of Pisa, he switched to teaching geometry and astronomy at the University of Padua. He also gave private lessons to students.

During the years he worked as a professor, Galileo kept experimenting with motion and forces. He made scientific discoveries about motion and falling objects that would not be published for another thirty to forty years. During this same time, he invented a pump, a primitive thermometer, and a compass. As he studied the tides, Galileo slowly came to agree with the Copernican theory that Earth rotated around the sun, instead of the other way around, which is what most people believed at the time. He kept his theories secret, however. This was because he knew that the heliocentric (sun-centered, as opposed to geocentric, or Earth-centered) universe theory opposed scripture and the beliefs of the Catholic Church. Disagreeing with the Church and the members of the Inquisition (a Church investigative committee that enforced traditional religious beliefs) was not only dangerous to one's career and reputation. It could also be fatal.

## KEEPING AN EYE ON THE SKY

In 1609, Galileo learned about something that would change the rest of his life. He heard about a spyglass invented by a Dutch scientist that allowed a person to see farther than usual. He studied it and then made his own version, grinding and polishing the lenses himself. His model was an improvement over the original. He called it the *perspicillum* (Latin for spectacles or glasses). It later became known as a telescope.

At first, Galileo thought his telescope would best be used by ships at sea and by the military. By the end of 1609, however, he was no longer using the invention to gaze at the horizon. Instead, Galileo was now using his telescope to search the stars and planets overhead. He found that seeing farther into the night sky allowed him to learn more about the way the universe worked than anything else ever had. He learned a great deal in just a matter of months, including the fact that there were mountains on the moon and celestial bodies orbiting around Jupiter. Many of these findings were published in 1610 in his book *Starry Messenger*.

Galileo kept up his observations. He verified that Venus went through phases just like the moon does, indicating that it revolves around the sun. This added further proof to the Copernican theory of the heliocentric universe. As Galileo's theories became more widely known, he began to be treated like a celebrity in many parts of Europe. He gave speeches, and banquets were held in his honor. Even as people began to accept and appreciate his surprising and revolutionary findings, the Catholic Church was becoming more and more concerned. It was worried about the fact that these findings did not conform to scripture's notion of a geocentric universe—the idea that all of creation revolved around Earth and, by extension, mankind. In 1616, Pope Paul V sent a warning to Galileo at his home ordering him to stop supporting Copernicus's theories in his written works, speeches, and presentations.

# The Formula for Speed

The actual formula for speed can appear rather intimidating when you first look at it. It helps to apply it to something you can easily understand. For example, the formula reads:

Speed = (distance traveled) / (time to travel that distance)

So, if you rode your bike from your house to your school, you can figure out your speed this way:

Speed = (15 miles [24 km]) / (1 ½ hours)
Therefore, Speed = 10 miles per hour (16 km per hour)

You can use this formula to figure out everything from how hard you kick the soccer ball to how fast you run around a track. Next time you take the dog for a walk, ride in the car to visit your aunt Clara, or walk from one classroom to the next, use the formula to figure out just how fast or slow you are moving.

## THE MAN WHO FELL TO EARTH

In 1624, Galileo met with Pope Urban VIII (who succeeded Paul V in 1621) and a number of Church cardinals. They told him that he could continue to develop and publish his theories as long as he treated them as math formulas only—not as declared truths about life and existence. For the next six years, Galileo labored over his greatest work, *Dialogue Concerning the Two Chief World Systems*. He was instructed to send the preface and conclusion of the book to the Church's censors for review and "correction." The rest of the book was to be sent to the Inquisition for approval.

In this painting by the nineteenth-century artist Cristiano Banti, Galileo is seen defending himself in front of the Inquisition court. In reality, he was probably not physically well enough to stand and face them with this much defiance and energy.

Approval was not given. Instead, Galileo was summoned to meet with the Inquisitor. The scientist sent a message that he was too ill to travel, but his plea was rejected. He was ordered to appear in Rome immediately or be brought there in chains. In April 1633, Galileo was interrogated by the Inquisition for days. When it was over, the two sides plea bargained. If Galileo admitted to being too supportive of Copernicus's theories and promised to say so in his next book, the Inquisition would give him a lesser charge. Galileo was found guilty of heresy and sentenced to prison. This sentence was soon changed to lifelong house arrest. His *Dialogue* was banned, and he was forbidden to publish any new work. Galileo was also forced to recant (deny) his theories on the heliocentric universe. Despite his recantation, Galileo remained unbowed. While under house arrest, his last book, *Discourse on Two New Sciences*, was smuggled out of Italy and published in Holland. It dealt with his theories about centers of gravity, acceleration, and inclined planes.

In 1638, at the age of seventy-four, Galileo was completely blind. He petitioned the Inquisition to be freed from house arrest, but his request was denied. Finally, in January 1642, he died. It took 350 years for the Church to formally declare that Galileo had in fact been correct about the heliocentric universe, and the Inquisition verdict was wrong. This belated acknowledgment of both Galileo's genius and innocence was made by Pope John Paul II in 1992.

## An Unpromising Beginning

Isaac Newton was born in England just one year after Galileo's death in 1642. Much of his scientific work concerning motion and forces was based on Galileo's theories. In fact, Newton was once quoted as saying about the astronomer, "If I have seen farther than others, it is because I have stood on the shoulders of giants."

Newton's early life was a difficult one. His father died before he was born. When he was only two years old, he was sent to be raised by his grandparents. He was not happy there. He did not do well in school and left before completing his studies.

Newton was put in charge of handling his family's estate, a job for which he had no talent or love. Finally, he returned to school. This time around, he was successful, graduating at the very top of his class.

In 1661, at the age of eighteen, Newton entered the University of Cambridge's prestigious Trinity College to pursue a degree in law. He had already shown a strong mechanical aptitude, making new and improved models of machines like clocks and windmills. In between his other classes, Newton read the works of Copernicus, Galileo, and Johannes Kepler (1571-1630), a German mathematician and astronomer. This research prompted Newton to write and publish his own book of philosophical questions.

According to some stories, Newton's focus changed one day in 1663 when he happened to buy a trigonometry book at a fair in Cambridge. When he tried to read and understand it, he found it too difficult. He got an easier book and struggled with that one, too. So Newton obtained an even simpler and more basic book. This one he understood! He then began working forward toward the more difficult books, and his foundation of knowledge broadened and strengthened. Newton quickly discovered that mathematics was his passion—not the law.

In the spring of 1665, Newton earned his bachelor's degree from Cambridge. Although he planned to return to school for a more advanced degree, the university shut down. The plague was rippling across Europe, killing millions of people. For two years, Newton stayed at home, intensively researching the fields of optics, physics, mathematics, and astronomy. It was during this period that he began developing the foundation of what would eventually become his three laws of motion. They were based largely on the earlier work of Kepler and Galileo.

## FALLING APPLES AND SPINNING BODIES

When Cambridge University reopened in 1667, Newton returned to Trinity College and earned his master's degree the following year. One of the most impressive discoveries he made during this time was that white light—up until then thought to be an entity lacking color—was actually made up of a spectrum of colors. Using this discovery, Newton created a reflecting telescope. He also developed what came to be known as his gravitational theory. How he came up with it has become the stuff of legend, and no one is quite sure if the story is true.

According to the legend, Newton was walking in his garden one day when he decided to rest under an apple tree. While there, an apple fell on his head. It inspired him to think about how gravity worked on the

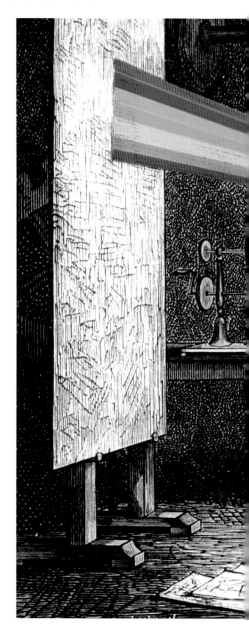

Newton's discovery, with the help of a prism, of the full spectrum of light contained within white light is depicted in this drawing from the mid-1750s.

apple. If gravity reached all the way to the top of the apple tree, could it go higher? Could it reach as high as the moon, for example? If so, that could prove that the orbit of the moon around Earth was due to gravitational forces.

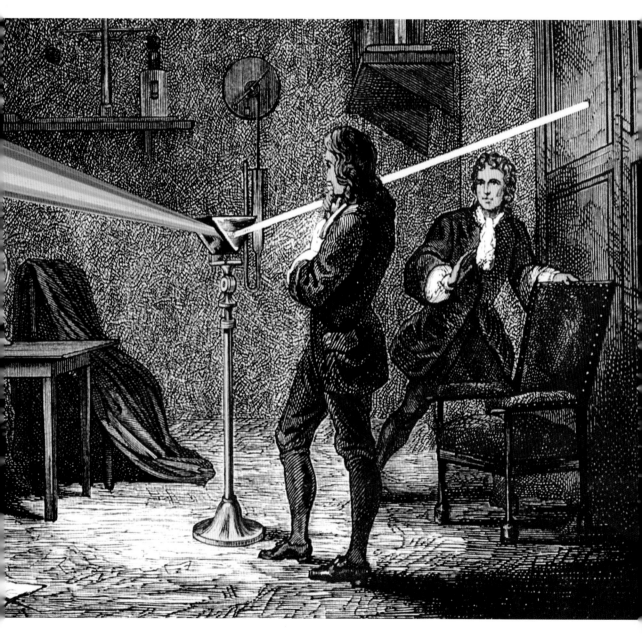

As a result of these musings, Newton developed the theory that stated, "All matter attracts all other matter with a force proportional to the product of their masses and inversely proportional to the square of the distance between them." What this basically means is that celestial bodies, like Earth and the moon, or the sun and Earth, are drawn to each other by gravity. The body with the larger mass exerts so much gravitational pull that it bends the linear path along which the smaller body travels. This bending results in the smaller body's circular or elliptical orbit around the larger body. This is why Earth rotates around the sun, and the moon orbits Earth. This gravitational force decreases—but still remains present—the farther away the bodies are from each other.

The actual details of the "Isaac Newton and the Falling Apple" story are most likely not factual. Yet walking around the family farm might be where Newton first began thinking about and working out his theory. In 1687, Newton published his gravitational theories in a book entitled *Mathematical Principles of Natural Philosophy*. Today, the book is still considered one of the most important scientific texts ever to be published. It changed how people looked at the world around them. Newton's ideas explained many natural and celestial phenomena that were still total mysteries. These included the orbits of comets and planets, how the ocean tides waxed and waned, and the motions and phases of the moon.

## A Retreat from Science and Celebrity

Despite all that he had learned and discovered, Newton struggled to cope with his new celebrity. He was frequently torn between the fame and recognition that his theories could bring and the criticism and commentary that they could also attract. After someone accused him of stealing ideas in 1678, he had a nervous breakdown. As time passed, he withdrew from his colleagues more and more. In 1693, Newton had another breakdown and decided to cease any further research. Some biographies say this emotional instability was due to illness or chemical poisoning, while others say it was deep depression.

Whatever the reason, Newton put teaching, studying, researching, and writing behind him and took a job with the English government. He became quite wealthy. Over the following years, he was elected and reelected president of the Royal Society. In 1705, he was knighted by Queen Anne, the first scientist ever to receive that honor. He passed away in 1727 at the age of eighty-four.

## OTHER PHYSICISTS OF NOTE

Although Galileo and Newton are two of the most important scientists to contribute ideas and knowledge to the world of physics, there have been others throughout the centuries. Two Germans, Hermann von Helmholtz (1821–1894) and Rudolf Clausius (1822–1888), developed the first and second laws of thermodynamics. K. Eric Drexler (b. 1955) popularized the field of nanotechnology, while Nathan Seiberg (b. 1956) contributed to the development of string theories. Charles Kuen Kao (b. 1933) from Hong Kong has done astounding work with fiber optics and the analysis of signal loss in communication cables.

As Newton so clearly stated and demonstrated, achievements and advances made in the understanding of physics

Charles Kuen Kao *(left)* receives the Nobel Prize in Physics from Swedish King Carl XVI Gustaf at the Concert Hall in Sweden in 2009. He received the award for his work in fiber optic communications.

(and all branches of science generally) rarely, if ever, come from one person alone. Instead, each innovator builds his or her theories and experiments on the work done by others. "Standing on the shoulders of giants," each person has contributed to a better, more thorough understanding of our planet and the universe.

# 4

# THE "MAGIC" OF MAGNETS

M agnets had been used for thousands of years before anyone had the faintest idea of how they worked. It wasn't until the twentieth century that scientists finally figured out the mysterious force that accounts for a magnet's ability to attract or repel other objects. Indeed, until scientists figured out what this force was and how it worked, magnets were seen as a type of unexplainable magic.

## MAGNETIC FIELDS AND POLES

The creation of a magnetic field can be observed when a magnet is placed on the same table as an iron nail. Slowly push the magnet across the table,

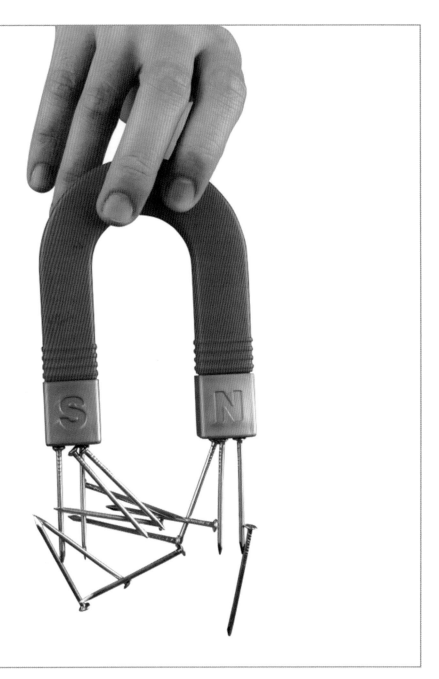

The way that magnets can pick up items that they are not in direct contact with can be explained by science and an understanding of the forces at work. Yet the power of magnets somehow still seems a little magical.

and at some point, the nail will seem to leap across the open space and attach itself to the magnet. This magnetic field can even penetrate through materials. This is why a magnet can hold up pieces of paper on a refrigerator door. The field reaches through paper to the metal of the door. A magnet can pick up several paper clips at once because the magnetic field it creates travels through each clip, magnetizing as it goes.

Magnets have two ends, referred to as poles. The magnet's north pole points toward Earth's North Pole, and the south pole to the planet's South Pole. Like poles repel (north pushes away north, south repels south), while unlike poles attract (north

## Exploring Perpetual Motion

The idea of creating a perpetual motion machine is one that has tantalized scientists and inventors since the Middle Ages. Who can blame them? Theoretically, such an invention should be possible. Imagine a machine that either keeps moving without ever slowing down or stopping or one that creates or generates more energy than it uses. The pursuit of this ideal has inspired countless inventions, none of which have been successful. Perhaps Sir Isaac Newton stated it best when he said, "The seekers after perpetual motion are trying to get something from nothing."

Some of the first examples of such an invention include a wheel created in India around 1150 CE, a self-blowing windmill, and even Leonardo da Vinci's "chimney jack," a machine used to turn a roasting skewer. Over the centuries, more and more inventors have tried to come up with some type of never-ending machine. Most modern inventors know that a perpetual motion machine is not possible. Everything runs down eventually, although it may take longer than a single lifetime to do so. Yet some keep trying to defeat the laws of nature and create one. In 2008, a Canadian inventor named Thane Heins claimed to have created such a machine, which he named Perepiteia. By the following year, experts and skeptics were already explaining how the device had failed to meet the requirements of a perpetual motion machine.

attracts south). Cut a magnet in half and each half will instantly have its own north and south poles.

## PRACTICAL USES FOR MAGNETS

Other than providing entertaining science activities, how does the force within magnets affect today's world? Magnets are used to make the electric motors and generators that run electric toothbrushes, lawn mowers, televisions, and furnaces. Magnets keep refrigerator doors closed. They read and write

The maglev train in Shanghai, China, is the world's only commercial maglev system. Experts suspect that more of these trains will be built throughout the world once the complications of installing them are solved.

digital information on computers' hard drives. Other common items that contain magnets include microwaves, credit cards, stereo speakers, and television coils. CD and DVD players use them, as well as garbage disposal motors, garage door openers, washers and dryers, windshield wipers, and can openers. Huge electromagnets are also used to sort metals in scrap yards. Compasses use magnets to show direction.

Maglev (magnetic levitation) technology places super-powerful magnets in train tracks. This allows trains to reach speeds of more than 300 miles (483 km) per hour, without the use of a fossil-fuel burning engine. The train actually floats 0.39 to 3.93 inches (1 to 10 centimeters) above the tracks. Floating along on a cushion of air created by the magnetic field, the train experiences no friction, so high speeds are easy to reach.

## MEDICAL MAGNETS

In recent years, magnets have also been used in the medical world. Some people believe that adding magnets to the insoles of shoes or within mattress frames can improve health. Although this type of treatment falls under the heading of alternative health, mainstream physicians also use magnets in X-rays and magnetic resonance imaging (MRI). Both of these techniques allow doctors to see inside the human body and learn more about how it functions and if there is a health problem of any kind. One of the largest MRI machines is found at the University of Illinois in Chicago. It is used to search the brain for possible diseases before symptoms even arise.

The strength of a magnet is measured in units called teslas. A refrigerator magnet is about 0.05 teslas. The magnet in the

University of Illinois MRI machine is 9.4 teslas and weighs 99,208 pounds (45 tons). There are only four MRI machines this large in the world. Large magnets are also being used in the operating room to work their way through a patient's heart during surgery in ways that physicians cannot.

## MAGNETS OF TOMORROW

Magnets play a large role in the European Organization for Nuclear Research's Large Hadron Collider (LHC) at the European

Soon after going into operation, the Large Hadron Collider set a record for high-energy collisions. Proton beams crashed into each other with three times more force than they ever had before.

Laboratory for Particle Physics near Geneva, Switzerland. It uses powerful magnets to produce magnetic fields. These magnetic fields will send protons, moving at almost the speed of light, into the right pathways inside the collider's 17-mile (27 km) long tunnel.

Many experiments on what magnets are capable of are being conducted at the Los Alamos Magnet Lab. Here experts are able, with a few flicks of various switches, to create a magnetic field more than a million times stronger than Earth's! The lab is experimenting with magnets to see how they can make buildings greener, gadgets smaller, and power and light systems more efficient.

Other possible future uses for magnets include hybrid cars that are powered by them and a magnetic radiation shielding system that protects astronauts on long interplanetary journeys. An MRI machine capable of detecting if a person is lying (based on distinctive patterns of brain activity) is being studied and may eventually be used as proof in the courtrooms of tomorrow.

# 5

# MOTION AND FORCES ON THE FAIRGROUNDS

Yorou climb in. The safety bar feels cold and hard against your shaking, sweating hands. It makes a clanging noise as it snaps into place across your lap. You glance at the nuts and bolts. They look tight—don't they? You can feel a rumble ripple from the first car back toward the one you sit in, and you know the time has finally come. After standing in line, waiting your turn, buying your ticket, and searching for a seat, your ride on the roller coaster is about to begin. You take a deep breath—it's the last one you take for the next four-and-a-half minutes.

The climb to the top of the first hill is agonizingly slow. The world seems to pause a moment just as you reach the top. And then you are hurtling 60 miles (97 km) an hour down a track you

While roller coasters are often challenging tests of the rider's courage and stomach, they are often even bigger physics challenges for the engineers who design them to be as safe as they are exciting.

are desperately hoping is in tiptop condition. You can see the upside-down loop coming up next, and you grasp the safety harness so hard your knuckles turn white. Why exactly did you voluntarily get on this "scream machine"?

Although physics is most likely not the first thing on your mind as your body careens around curves and plummets down slopes, you can bet that it was the number one consideration for the people who designed the ride. They are experts at using physics to simulate high-speed danger. They make sure

# Foucault's Pendulum

Have you ever gone to a science or university museum and seen a display that shows a pendulum ever so slowly tracing a full circle in the sand below it? It usually has a sign posted somewhere near it saying, "Foucault's Pendulum." Have you wondered what it was?

French physicist Jean-Bernard-Léon Foucault (1819–1868) was a man who liked investigating the world around him through experimentation. He was going to be a doctor but discovered that he could not stand the sight of blood, so that option was out. Next, he began learning as much as he could about different types of science, such as chemistry, electricity, and magnetism. Foucault eventually turned his attention to inventing a machine that could show people how Earth rotated on its axis. By the early 1850s, everyone had accepted the fact that Earth rotated on its axis. But Foucault wanted to use laboratory equipment to clearly demonstrate the phenomenon because he knew that not everyone had access to telescopes and other astronomical tools.

Foucault's first pendulum experiment was in his cellar. He used a heavy weight hung from the ceiling by a wire. When pulled back and released, the weight swung freely back and forth. It appeared to be moving back and forth along a straight and unvarying vertical plane, as it would do if the planet was motionless. Yet when studied carefully, it was observed that the plane of the pendulum's swing actually shifted about eleven degrees an hour. It completed a full circle in just over thirty-two hours. This rotation is due to Earth's own rotating movement beneath the pendulum.

Foucault improved upon his model and, a few years later, showed it off at the Paris Exhibition. The slow circles made in the sand by today's exhibits of Foucault's Pendulum illustrate the planet's rotation. Although many people continue to mistakenly assume that it is the pendulum that is rotating, it is actually the building—and the planet it is built upon—that is rotating and creating the circle. The pendulum merely swings, while Earth's rotation subtly curves the pendulum's otherwise vertical (straight) swinging movement.

that roller-coaster passengers feel like they are in far greater danger than they actually are.

## The Physics of Roller Coasters

How does a roller coaster use force to provide the thrills and chills of runaway speed? The first step in understanding this is to realize that a roller coaster does not have an engine. Once it has been pulled to the top of the first hill and begins its descent, it is propelled by momentum alone. Gravitational force has converted the potential energy of the coaster sitting still at the top of the first ascent into kinetic energy as it tips downhill. Once in motion, the roller coaster does not want to stop and won't as long as there is little friction. Friction is the enemy in this ride because that is what will slow the cars down (along with the compressed air brakes it uses at the very end, of course!). To reduce friction, special smooth wheels are used in building modern coasters. The fastest ones use steel for tracks, instead of wood, because the metal allows for steeper hills, more dramatic drops, and higher speeds.

Some of the newest roller coasters also rely heavily on the use of magnets. These types of coasters take off like a rocket, rather than making that first slow uphill climb. The roaring launch is due to magnetic propulsion, using magnets that repel each other to create the force. This magnetic propulsion is so strong that it can launch a coaster from 0 to 100 miles (0 to 161 km) an hour in seconds.

Many coasters also rely on magnets to do just the opposite—bring the rocketing ride to a halt. In this case, magnets that are attracted to each other slow down the cars until they come to a gentle stop. The first roller coaster to use magnets for a propulsive takeoff was the Flight of Fear, which began operating in 1996, at King's Island in Ohio. In 2000, the first magnetic brakes were used in the Millennium Force coaster at Cedar Point in Sandusky, Ohio. Now almost all coasters are built with magnet propulsion and braking systems. They are often referred to as hyper coasters.

## THINGS THAT GO BUMP IN THE NIGHT

Over at the bumper cars, Newton's third law of motion is running into walls left and right. To observe action-reaction at work, just jump on this ride for a little while. Clearly, colliding with a bumper car involves a lot less impact than crashing into a real car on the street. This is because the bumper cars are surrounded by a large rubber bumper. When the cars collide, the rubber helps absorb and diffuse (spread out) the force. The metal and plastic of real cars are poor at absorbing the force of impact. They usually

Bumper cars are an excellent way to watch forces and motion in action. Momentum, friction, inertia, and action-reaction are all on full display and on a collision course.

crumple without greatly diminishing the force of collision, which is why injuries to drivers and passengers are common and can be quite severe—even fatal.

What happens when two bumper cars collide? The two cars stop moving or change direction. Yet the inertia of the

drivers' bodies keeps them moving in the same direction and at the same speed as they were before the collision. That is why drivers' bodies jerk forward at the moment of collision—and why people suffer whiplash injuries in real car accidents. This is also why seat belts are so important in bumper cars and real automobiles. Without seat belts, drivers and passengers can be ejected from the vehicle (bumper car or real car) and go flying, leading to serious injury and, in the case of automobiles, death. How fast the bumper car is moving when it collides with another car—and how much mass each rider has—also affects the power of the bump.

## FREE FALLING

Remember Galileo? One of the experiments he performed was dropping items of different mass from the top of the Leaning Tower of Pisa to see how fast they would fall. This same principle is at work when someone buys a ticket for the free fall ride. Like the balls Galileo tested, in this type of ride, the passenger is moving solely under the power of gravity. Free fall rides are typically divided into three parts:

- The ride to the top
- The temporary suspension
- The plunging drop

Force provided by motors pushes the ride to the very top of the tower first. The amount of force used depends on the total mass of the car and the people sitting in it.

Next, the ride pauses at the top. There is no physics principle at work behind this dramatic pause—it is done merely to make the heart beat a little faster and the palms get a little sweatier. As the car suddenly drops, it accelerates toward the ground, thanks to gravity pulling on it. What slows and stops the plunging car? A special track is built into the ride that curves as it nears the ground, slowing the ride down. Once the car begins to slow, a brake is applied, bringing the ride to a complete and gentle halt.

## BACK AND FORTH, UP AND OVER

Pendulum rides are also driven by forces and motion. As passengers sit in one of these, swinging back and forth, they may start to experience a near-weightless feeling at the peak of the ride. If they happen to get on a pendulum ride that not only swings back and forth but actually does a complete 360-degree

Pendulum rides are popular at many amusement parks and county fairs. Many of them give riders the chance to feel what it would be like to be weightless—for at least a second anyway.

circle, they will definitely experience a brief "floating astronaut" moment. This weightless feeling is not due to a lessening of the forces of gravity. Instead, what the passengers feel is actually their own momentum acting against the force of gravity. As the riders reach the peak of the pendulum, their bodies are no longer fully in contact with their seats. Their momentum has in effect pushed them up and off. This helps riders feel—at least for a very brief moment—like they are weightless.

A day at the fair typically means a lot of sun, a lot of snacks, and a lot of fun. The next time you go, you can add one other item to the list: a lot of physics.

**acceleration** An increase in velocity.

**electromagnet** A device consisting of a conductive metal core that is magnetized by an electric current in a coil that surrounds it.

**fiber optics** A branch of optics that deals with the transmission of light through transparent fibers. (Optics is the branch of physics that studies the behavior and properties of light, including light's interaction with matter. Optics also refers to the construction of instruments that use or detect light.)

**friction** Surface resistance to relative motion.

**gravity** The force of attraction by which objects tend to fall or be pulled toward the center of Earth.

**heresy** A belief, opinion, or theory that is strongly at odds with traditional and conventional religious teachings.

**inertia** The property by which matter retains its state of rest or its velocity along a straight line as long as it is not acted upon by an external force.

**Inquisition** An institution of the Roman Catholic Church designed to identify, combat, and suppress heresy.

**Large Hadron Collider** The world's largest high-energy particle accelerator.

**maglev** Term for "magnetic levitation," which is used in transportation systems such as high-speed trains.

**magnetic field** A field of force produced by a magnetic object or particle. A magnetic field extends infinitely and is present whether or not it is acting on another object.

**momentum** The product of mass multiplied by velocity.

**pendulum** A body suspended from a fixed support so that it swings freely back and forth under the influence of gravity.

**petition** To officially request or ask something of someone, usually an official or a government, organization, or other powerful institution.

**physics** The science of matter and energy and the interactions between the two.

**poles** The two opposing ends of magnets. When freely suspended, the end that points toward Earth's North Pole is referred to as the magnet's north pole. Its other end is referred to as its south pole. The north pole of Magnet A will be attracted to the south pole of Magnet B, while Magnet A's north pole will repel Magnet B's north pole, just as Magnet A's south pole will repel Magnet B's south pole.

**reflecting telescope** A type of telescope that uses a concave mirror to gather light from the object being viewed and focus it on an adjustable eyepiece or lenses.

**string theories** Hypotheses describing elementary particles as tiny one-dimensional objects rather than zero-dimensional points.

**thermodynamics** The science concerned with the relations between heat and mechanical energy or work and the conversion of one into the other.

**vector** A quantity with both magnitude and direction.

**American Association for the Advancement of Science**

1200 New York Avenue NW

Washington, DC 20005

(202) 326-6400

Web site: http://www.aaas.org

A 150-year old international organization, this group works to promote and advance all fields of science by fostering education, enhancing communication, promoting science and its uses, and increasing public involvement.

**American Institute of Physics**

One Physics Ellipse

College Park, MD 20740-3843

(301) 209-3100

Web site: http://www.aip.org

This organization is dedicated to promoting advancements and education in the field of physics. It provides helpful information for scientists, students, and the general public.

**Canada Science and Technology Museum**

P.O. Box 9724, Station T

Ottawa, ON K1G 5A3

Canada

(613) 991-3044

Web site: http://www.sciencetech.technomuses.ca/english
The largest of its kind in Canada, this museum fulfills its mission of helping the public better understand the ongoing relationships between science, technology, and society—and the resulting transformation of Canada—through its collection; permanent, temporary, and traveling exhibits; special events; school programs; workshops and demonstrations; publications; loans; conferences and lectures; expert advice; and joint action with other museums and organizations with similar goals and interests.

**Canadian Association of Physicists**
MacDonald Building, Suite 112
University of Ottawa
150 Louis Pasteur Private
Ottawa, ON K1N 6N5
Canada
(613) 562-5614
Web site: http://www.cap.ca/en
A resource for teachers, students, and scientists alike, this organization offers lecture tours, conferences, and competitions.

**Fermilab**
P.O. Box 500
Batavia, IL 60510-5011
(630) 840-3000
Web site: http://www.fnal.gov
This well-known lab conducts basic research into all elements

of particle physics and has the world's second highest energy particle accelerator in the world.

## Institute of Physics (IOP)

76 Portland Place

London, England W1B 1NT

44 (9) 7470 4800

Web site: http://www.iop.org

The IOP is a leading professional organization working to promote developments in physics. Its Web site includes information about conferences, research, and other topics in the field.

## Isaac Newton Institute for Mathematical Sciences

20 Clarkson Road

Cambridge, England CB3 0EH

44 (0)1223 335999

Web site: http://www.newton.ac.uk

The Isaac Newton Institute for Mathematical Sciences is a national and international visitor research institute. It runs research programs on selected themes in mathematics and the mathematical sciences with applications over a wide range of science and technology. It attracts leading mathematical scientists from England and overseas to collaborate on research over an extended period.

## National Science Foundation

4201 Wilson Boulevard

Arlington, VA 22230

(703) 292-5111

Web site: http://www.nsf.gov

This federal agency was created by Congress in 1950 to "promote the progress of science; to advance the national
health, prosperity, and welfare; and to secure the national
defense." It supports all fields within fundamental science
and engineering.

## WEB SITES

Due to the changing nature of Internet links, Rosen
Publishing has developed an online list of Web sites related to
the subject of this book. This site is updated regularly. Please
use this link to access this list:

http://www.rosenlinks.com/sms/maf

# FOR FURTHER READING

Basher, Simon, and Dan Green. *Physics: Why Matter Matters!* New York, NY: Kingfisher, 2008.

Davila, Adrienne. *Move It!: Motion, Forces, and You*. Tonawanda, NY: Kids Can Press, 2005.

DeRosa, Tom, and Carolyn Reeves. *Forces and Motion: From High-Speed Jets to Wind-Up Toys*. Green Forest, AR: New Leaf Publishing Group, 2009.

DiSpezio, Michael. *Awesome Experiments in Force and Motion*. New York, NY: Sterling, 2006.

Gardner, Robert. *Forces and Motion Science Fair Projects: Using the Scientific Method*. Berkeley Heights, NJ: Enslow Publishers, 2010.

Hollihan, Kerrie Logan. *Isaac Newton and Physics for Kids: His Life and Ideas with 21 Activities*. Chicago, IL: Chicago Review Press, 2009.

Lepora, Nathan. *The Science Behind Thrill Rides*. Strongsville, OH: Gareth Stevens, 2008.

Monroe, Tilda. *What Do You Know About Forces and Motion?* New York, NY: PowerKids Press, 2010.

Nardo, Don. *Force and Motion: Laws of Movement*. Mankato, MN: Compass Point Books, 2008.

Newton, Jane. *Gravity in Action: Roller Coasters!* New York, NY: PowerKids Press, 2009.

Oxlade, Chris. *Forces and Motion: An Investigation*. New York, NY: PowerKids Press, 2008.

Panchyk, Richard. *Galileo for Kids: His Life and Ideas with 25 Activities*. Chicago, IL: Chicago Review Press, 2005.

Robinson, Richard. *Forces and Movement*. Mankato, MN: QEB Publishing, 2008.

Solway, Andrew. *Exploring Forces and Motion*. New York, NY: Rosen Publishing Group, 2007.

Uttley, Colin. *Experiments with Force and Motion*. Strongsville, OH: Gareth Stevens, 2010.

Weir, Jane. *Forces and Motion*. Mankato, MN: Compass Point Books, 2009.

Welch, Catherine A. *Forces and Motion: A Question and Answer Book*. Mankato, MN: Capstone Press, 2007.

Whiting, Jim. *The Science of Hitting a Home Run: Forces and Motion in Action*. Mankato, MN: Capstone Press, 2010.

# BIBLIOGRAPHY

Basher, Simon, and Dan Green. *Physics: Why Matter Matters!* New York, NY: Kingfisher, 2008.

Ellis-Christensen, Tricia. "How Are Magnets Used in Roller Coasters?" WiseGeek.com, 2010. Retrieved April 2010 (http://www.wisegeek.com/how-are-magnets-used-in-roller-coasters.htm).

Ellis-Christensen, Tricia. "What Is a Hyper Coaster?" WiseGeek.com. Retrieved April 2010 (http://www.wisegeek.com/what-is-a-hyper-coaster.htm).

Encyclopedia Smithsonian. "Foucault Pendulum." SI.edu. Retrieved April 2010 (http://www.si.edu/Encyclopedia_SI/nmah/pendulum.htm).

Groleau, Rick. "Galileo's Battle for the Heavens: His Experiments." PBS.org, 2002. Retrieved April 2010 (http://www.pbs.org/wgbh/nova/galileo/experiments.html).

Hall, Alfred Rupert, and Microsoft Encarta. "Isaac Newton's Life." Isaac Newton Institute for Mathematical Sciences, 1998. Retrieved April 2010 (http://www.newton.ac.uk/newtlife.html).

Hoadley, Rick. "Cool Experiments with Magnets." CoolMagnetMan.com, 2008. Retrieved April 2010 (http://www.coolmagnetman.com).

Jezek, Geno. "How Magnets Work!" HowMagnetsWork.com, 2006. Retrieved April 2010 (http://www.howmagnetswork.com).

Kahan, Peter. *Science Explorer: Motion, Forces, and Energy.* Upper Saddle River, NJ: Prentice Hall, 2000.

Krumenaker, Larry, and Pamela J. W. Gore. "Forces and Motion: Newton's Laws of Motion." Georgia Perimeter College, 2007. Retrieved April 2010 (http://facstaff.gpc.edu/~pgore/PhysicalScience/forces-motion.html).

Learner.org. "Amusement Park Physics: What Are the Forces Behind the Fun?" Retrieved April 2010 (http://www.learner.org/interactives/parkphysics/index.html).

LearningScience.org. "Motion and Forces." Retrieved April 2010 (http://www.learningscience.org/psc2bmotionforces.htm).

Lienhard, John H. H. "Engines of Our Ingenuity: No. 166: Galileo's Experiment." University of Houston. Retrieved April 2010 (http://www.uh.edu/engines/epi166.htm).

Louviere, Georgia. "Newton's Laws of Motion." 2006. Retrieved April 2010 (http://teachertech.rice.edu/Participants/louviere/Newton).

O'Connor, J. J., and E. F. Robertson. "Galileo Galilei." School of Mathematics and Statistics, University of St. Andrew's, 2002. Retrieved April 2010 (http://www-history.mcs.st-and.ac.uk/Biographies/Galileo.html).

Physics4Kids.com. "Motion." Retrieved April 2010 (http://www.physics4kids.com/files/motion_intro.html).

Robertson, William C. *Force and Motion.* Arlington, VA: NSTA Press, 2002.

Science Online. "Force and Motion." Retrieved April 2010 (http://classroom.jc-schools.net/sci-units/force.htm).

ThinkQuest.org. "Force and Motion." Retrieved April 2010 (http://library.thinkquest.org/CR0215468/force_and_motion.htm).

# INDEX

## ABOUT THE AUTHOR

Tamra Orr is the author of many nonfiction books for students. She received her bachelor's degree in English and Secondary Education from Ball State University in Muncie, Indiana. Orr lives in the Pacific Northwest with her four children, one husband, one cat, and one dog. With all of these bodies in constant motion, Orr has had the opportunity to study forces and motion at work, up close, every day.

## PHOTO CREDITS